The
Do-It-Yourself
Drawing Book

Anna Burgess

Illustrated by Kim Gamble

Watermill Press

The Do-It-Yourself Drawing Book
First published in the United States by Watermill Press,
an imprint of Troll Associates, Inc.

Text copyright © 1994 by Anna Burgess.
Illustrations copyright © 1994 by Anna Burgess and
Lineup Pty Limited.

Design by Kim Gamble

Burgess, Anna.
  The do-it-yourself drawing book.

 ISBN 0-8167-3626-X
Printed in the United States of America.

10 9 8 7 6 5 4 3

  1. Drawing - Technique - Juvenile literature. I. Gamble, Kim.
  II. Title.

741.2

BECOME A
DO-IT-YOURSELF ARTIST

an you draw?
You can, you know. Everyone can. And everyone can learn to draw better. Even if you only draw stick figures, that's a start.

In fact, **The Do-It-Yourself Drawing Book** is just what you need to get your artwork really humming! To be good at anything – say, playing guitar or rapping or playing ball – you have to practice. If you practice, you'll become a good artist – maybe even a great artist!

The Do-It-Yourself Drawing Book is for dipping into. Flick through it and find a section that interests you. Try it. You'll get ideas from the pages. Experiment with these ideas, and you'll learn new skills. You'll have fun. Your drawings will get better, too. This will help you at school, but remember that having fun is what art is really all about.

Become a do-it-yourself artist today!

P.S. *Bookworm knows about some pretty famous artists. Sometimes, he loves to name drop. Use the library if you want to know who he's talking about!*

CONTENTS

	Page
The Best Tool – Your Very Own Sketchbook	5
What Other Tools Do I Need?	6
Getting a Different Angle on It	8
Keep It in Proportion	12
Putting It Together	14
Where There's Light, There's Dark	16
Figuring Out Figures	20
Sticking With It	21
Scribbling Is the Way to Go	22
Shaping Up	23
Is There a Skeleton in Your Closet?	24
It's Not Only Skin Deep	26
Drawing It How It *Isn't*	28
Let's Face It!	29
The Eyes Have It	32
Hair! Hair!	34
Do It With Feeling	35
I've Got to Hand It to You!	36
Listening to Hands	37
Put Your Foot Down!	38
Put Your Foot in It!	39
Fruity Shapes	40
Eat Your Veggies	42
How to Treat Trees	44
Million-Dollar Flowers	46
Escape Into Landscape	48
Cityscapes	50
Animals Are People Too!	52
Don't Horse Around!	54
It's All in the Folds	56
Models That Don't Move	57
Trains & Planes & Boats & Cars	58
Move It Right Along!	63

THE BEST TOOL –
YOUR VERY OWN SKETCHBOOK

If you're going to be an artist, you'll want your own sketchbook. It can be any kind of book you like. All you need are blank pages to draw on. Your sketchbook goes everywhere with you. EVERYWHERE? Well, almost. You never know when you'll want to sketch something interesting.

A sketch is a quick drawing. A rough drawing. It's a bit like a note to remind you how something looks in case you want to draw it later. You can record details that you might forget in your sketchbook.

Later, at home or at school, you can use your sketches to help you draw.

Sketch quickly. It's never perfect. It's not meant to be. You'll get better with practice.

So what might a page in your sketchbook look like?

Here's a sample page from mine....

KEEP A SHARP PENCIL OR TWO ALWAYS ON HAND!

Magnolia – Dk green, pale green veins

Gran's table

pups ear, back view

front view.

feet.

Looking down on Sylvester.

WHAT OTHER TOOLS DO I NEED?

You can draw anywhere. You can draw in sand with a stick, but I suggest you get hold of some pencils, crayons, and paper – and, of course, your *very own sketchbook.*

Artists use all sorts of different materials for their drawings. They call these materials "media" or "mediums."
You might use some of these mediums:

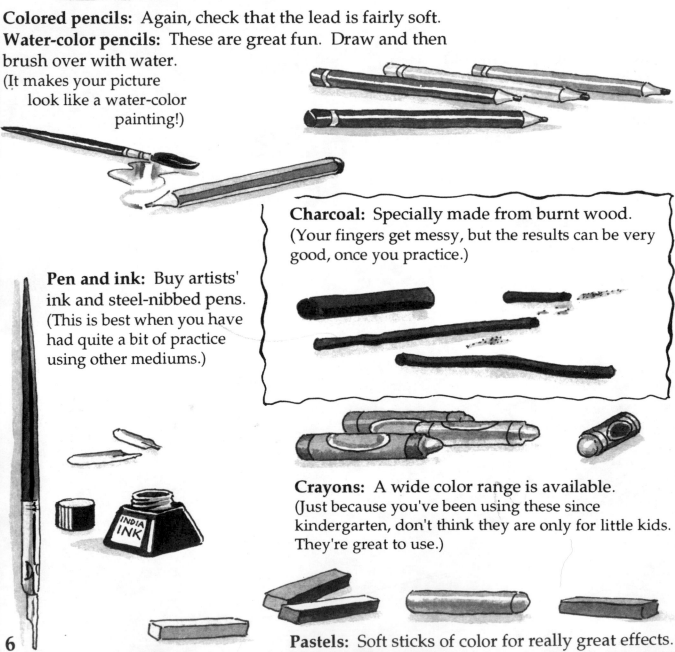

Black lead pencils: Go for the softer ones, the ones with "B" labels. (HB to 6B – the higher the number, the softer the lead.)

Colored pencils: Again, check that the lead is fairly soft.
Water-color pencils: These are great fun. Draw and then brush over with water.
(It makes your picture look like a water-color painting!)

Charcoal: Specially made from burnt wood. (Your fingers get messy, but the results can be very good, once you practice.)

Pen and ink: Buy artists' ink and steel-nibbed pens. (This is best when you have had quite a bit of practice using other mediums.)

Crayons: A wide color range is available. (Just because you've been using these since kindergarten, don't think they are only for little kids. They're great to use.)

Pastels: Soft sticks of color for really great effects.

Take a 3B pencil and try these different effects:

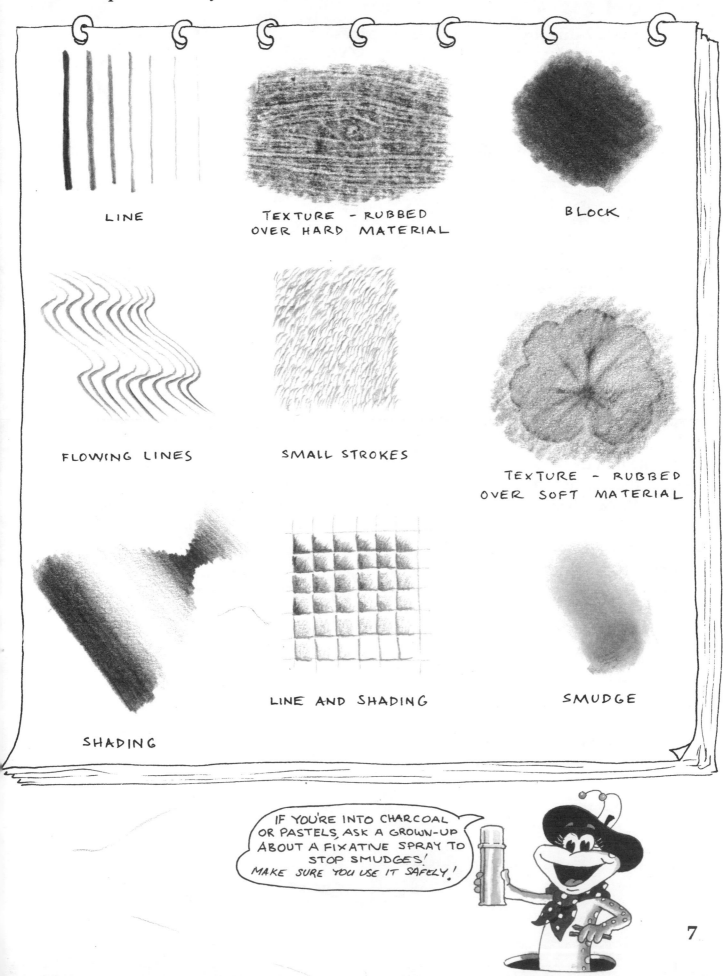

LINE

TEXTURE - RUBBED
OVER HARD MATERIAL

BLOCK

FLOWING LINES

SMALL STROKES

TEXTURE - RUBBED
OVER SOFT MATERIAL

SHADING

LINE AND SHADING

SMUDGE

IF YOU'RE INTO CHARCOAL
OR PASTELS, ASK A GROWN-UP
ABOUT A FIXATIVE SPRAY TO
STOP SMUDGES!
MAKE SURE YOU USE IT SAFELY!

GETTING A DIFFERENT ANGLE ON IT

You can do 2-dimensional drawings, like these:

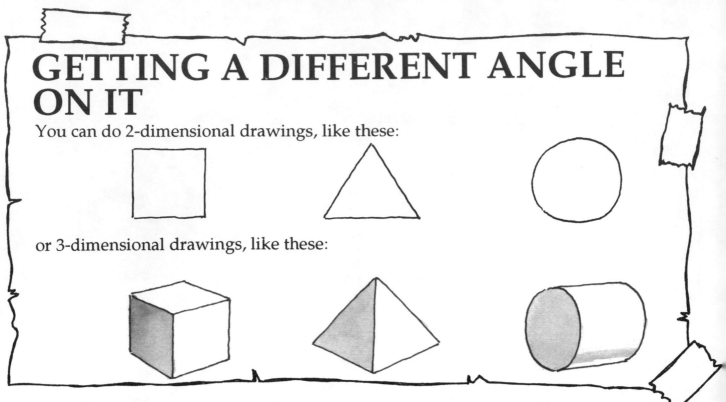

or 3-dimensional drawings, like these:

Adding the third dimension gives your drawing depth. It's easy to get a 3-D effect, once you understand "perspective."

• Imagine there's a big, solid block of wood way in front of you, level with your eyes and you are looking at it through a big, clear sheet of plastic. This represents what is called the "picture plane."

• Imagine that there is a dotted line across the plastic at the level of your eyes. We call this the "horizon line."

• The sides of the block in the distance seem to be sloping toward the horizon line.

• If we were to continue these lines until they all met (converged) on our horizon line, we'd have what we call "vanishing points."

This is perspective.

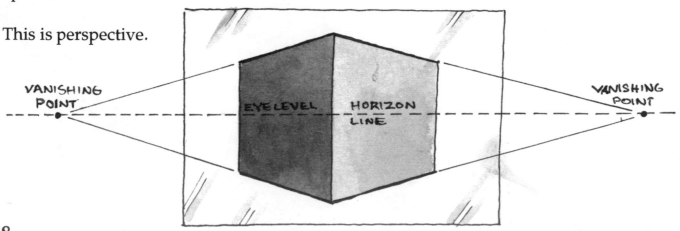

Perspective is different depending on which angle you're looking from. If you are looking *up* at the block, its perspective would be different from if you were looking *down* on it.

• Always start from the straight up and down (vertical) edge nearest to you.

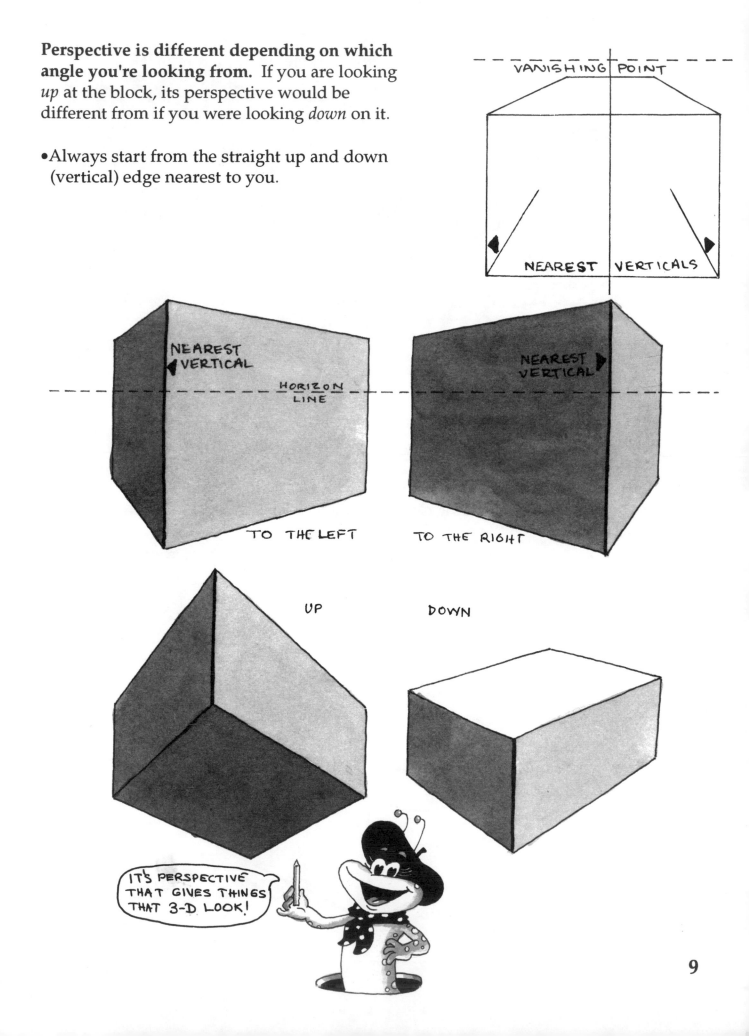

VANISHING POINT

NEAREST VERTICALS

NEAREST VERTICAL

HORIZON LINE

NEAREST VERTICAL

TO THE LEFT

TO THE RIGHT

UP

DOWN

IT'S PERSPECTIVE THAT GIVES THINGS THAT 3-D LOOK!

PERSPECTIVE

Once you've got the idea of perspective, you can try drawing a house.
Look at the house and imagine your "picture plane" – your imaginary
sheet of clear plastic with its horizon line. "Frame" your picture in it.

Decide which is the vertical line nearest to you. See how the lines *above*
the horizon slope down and away, and those *below* the horizon slope up
and away? These lines are really parallel lines. They are the same distance
apart, but look to be getting closer together the further they are from you
until they meet on the horizon line.

The best way to master perspective is to use old copies of magazines or newspapers.

- Take some tracing paper, a ruler, and a pencil.
- Look at a picture of a building or the inside of a room and find the eye-level or horizon.
- Draw a broken line to show the horizon.
- Draw over the nearest vertical line and sketch in all of the other parallel lines until they converge on the horizon line.
- Where the lines converge is the vanishing point.

HORIZON ————— ————— HORIZON

As you practice perspective, you'll find you are looking at everything with new eyes! You can experiment with perspective at home.

- Take a bowl and look at it from every angle. See how the perspective changes when you hold the bowl at different angles and heights.

Perspective means that distant objects seem smaller than close ones. The farther away an object is, the less detail you can see.

NOW YOU'RE EXAGGERATING!

11

KEEP IT IN PRoPORtIoN

Proportion is about getting the right size compared with other nearby objects.
If a puppy is beside a car, then you'll draw the puppy much smaller than the car.

As you use your sketchbook, keep an eye on proportions.
- Say you want to draw a cat, a kitten, a basket, and a ball of wool.

- Take a soft pencil.
- Draw three loose ovals, one about the right size for the cat and one for the kitten.

- Now draw in the details.
- You might need to use different basic shapes, depending on what you are drawing.

Keep checking. Should this be a bit larger?
A bit smaller? You can use your pencil as a great
tool for getting proportion right.

•Close one eye. Hold your pencil in front of you
  and move your thumb up and down to
  "measure" the height of things you want to
  draw.

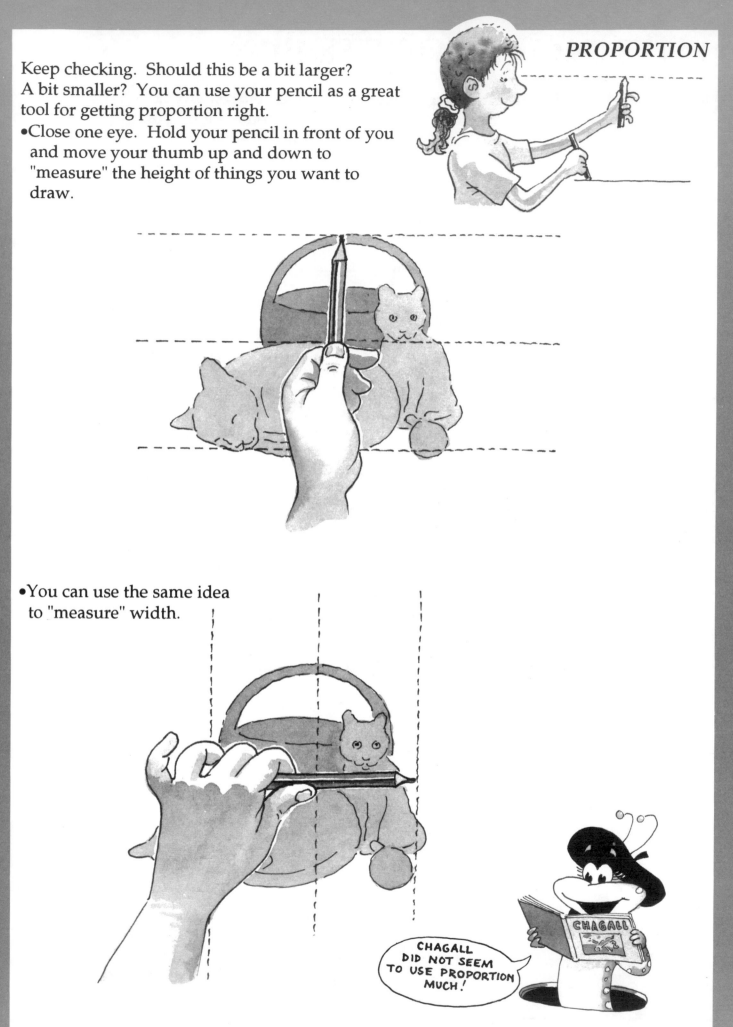

•You can use the same idea
  to "measure" width.

CHAGALL
DID NOT SEEM
TO USE PROPORTION
MUCH!

CHAGALL

PUTTING IT TOGETHER

When you take a photograph, you move the camera and yourself around until the picture you see in the frame looks just the way you want it. You are "composing" your picture. Composition is really important when you are drawing.

Composing Your Picture

First decide if your picture looks best horizontal (landscape)

or vertical (portrait).
•Use your hands to help you decide.

•You can make a rectangular view-frame out of cardboard.

•To compose your picture, first choose its shape.

•Choose something you think is important and put it near the center of your picture. See how picture A seems to "draw your eye" into the center of the picture?

A great thing about being an artist is that you can draw things just the way you want them.

- Look at the pictures below. The first one shows what the scene actually looked like. Yet see what you can do by adding some tree branches!

- If you want to put lots of things in your scene, try planning it first on graph paper. Then copy it section by section onto another lightly gridded sheet. You can add detail as you go.

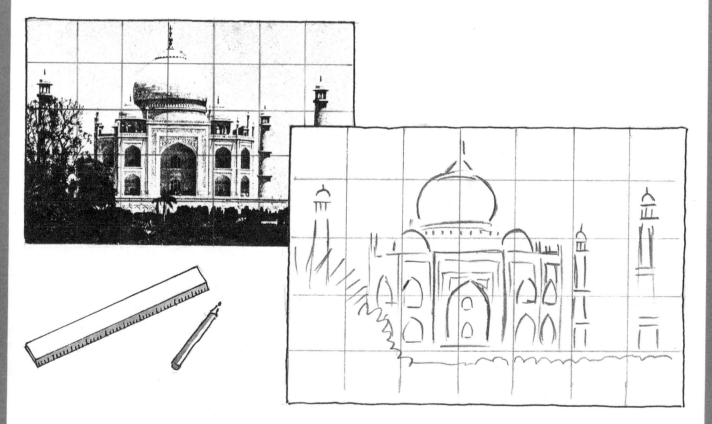

- Try putting the main feature of a picture to one side.
- You may want to add something to balance it. Try sketching lots of different compositions. You'll know you've got the composition right when it looks right to you!

WHERE THERE'S LIGHT, THERE'S DARK

Stand on a sidewalk on a sunny day, with your back to the sun. You'll see your shadow in front of you. Your body blocks some of the sun's rays, and you'll see a darker patch (or shadow) in the shape of your body.

Shadows

Whether it's the sun or a lamp that's the source of light, you'll get shadows. If the light is very strong, you'll get very dark shadows. If the light is weaker, you'll get soft shadows.

In drawing, use shading to show shape and depth. Shadows help make things seem real and can add feeling to your pictures.

The secret is to first find your "light source." Look at the object. Where is the light coming from? From a window? From the sun? From a lamp? From a camp fire?

• Start indoors. Choose any object that is there. Look for the light source. (Sometimes it helps to half close your eyes when you're checking for the light source.)

• Once you find the light source, you'll see that shadows are *always* on the side opposite that source.

• Study the shape of the object. Then study the shape of the shadow. Different shapes can create different shadows.

If a shadow hits a wall, you'll see it creates an angle.

Outside, the sun is usually the light source. As it moves across the sky (or appears to!) shadows change.
• Check out shadows early in the morning when the sun is low. What happens at midday when the sun is high in the sky? How do the shadows change as the sun sinks?

To get a feeling for the length of shadows, try this.

• Draw your object. Draw the sun.
• Sketch a line from the sun to the object to the ground. That shows how long the shadow will be.

LIGHT SOURCE

Once you've got the idea, you can start practicing.
•Get a few objects of different shapes.
•Arrange them on a sheet of white paper.
•Place a lamp to one side and above the objects.
•Sketch the objects and their shadows in pencil.

Now arrange the same objects, but make the
light source down near the table.
(A flashlight will do.)

•Sketch the objects and the new shadows.

Pencils are a good medium for showing
shadows, but there are different ways of
shading such as using pen and ink or fine-
tipped pens.

Sometimes the texture (or surface) of the
object will give you a hint as to which
medium you should use.

•Choose something soft and shade it with charcoal.

18

•Choose something hard and shiny and use pen and ink.

•Choose something textured and try crayon.

•Add shading in the background just to bring out the shape of an object.

CAVE DWELLERS WERE USING SHADING 30,000 YEARS AGO!

FIGURING OUT FIGURES

We're not talking about math figures, but human figures.
Drawing people looks hard (and it is), but with practice, you'll become
quite an expert! On the following pages there are some really useful tips
for getting the human shape right.

Proportions

When you look at people, notice the sizes of different parts of their bodies.
Some people have long legs compared with their height. Some people
have broad shoulders compared with their arm length. These comparisons
are called "proportions." The proportions of bodies are different for babies,
children, and adults.

•Stand in front of a full-length mirror and study your own proportions. Is
 your head about one-fifth of your height? How far down your thighs do
 your fingertips reach? Is this the same for an adult?

•Study people and
 then start sketching
 them.
•Look at details such
 as the length of their
 fingertips or arms.
•Think about those
 proportions.

MICHELANGELO
WAS GREAT WHEN
IT CAME TO PUTTING
PEOPLE ON CEILINGS!

STICKING WITH IT

Start drawing people by using "stick figures."

•Ask a friend to model for you while you sketch.

Sketch your stick figure:

•Use lines and circles to show how the person is standing (or sitting or lying).

•Use a soft pencil and just lightly sketch. (You'll want to erase these lines when you've finished with them.)

Flesh it out:

•Roughly sketch in the body outline.

Dress it up:

•Draw the clothes the person has on. (You can use whatever medium you choose. See page 56, "It's All in the Folds.")

SCRIBBLING IS THE WAY TO GO

Scribbling is a great way to start drawing bodies.
- Scribble circles and ovals until you get the proportions and the shapes right.
- Use a very soft pencil and make your lines free and loose.

- Ask a friend to model for you. Do lots of quick sketches showing different poses (or positions).

Scribbling is especially good for showing movement.
- Flesh out the scribble and then draw your outlines.

You'll finish your drawing in no time.

SHAPING UP

Another approach is to use just three basic shapes to make your figure:

cylinders (of various kinds)   **balls**   **cones**

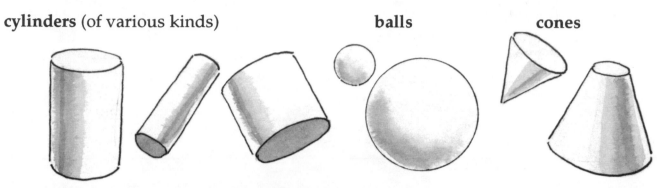

- Choose the best shapes to represent different parts of the body.
- Sketch these in, using a soft medium. Keep the right proportions in mind.

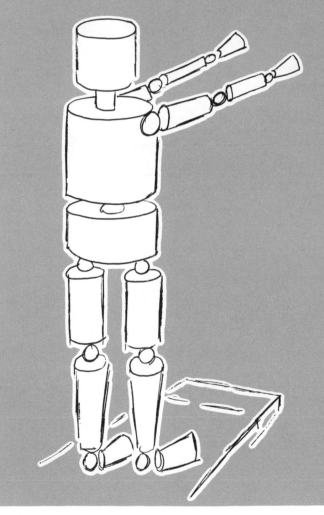

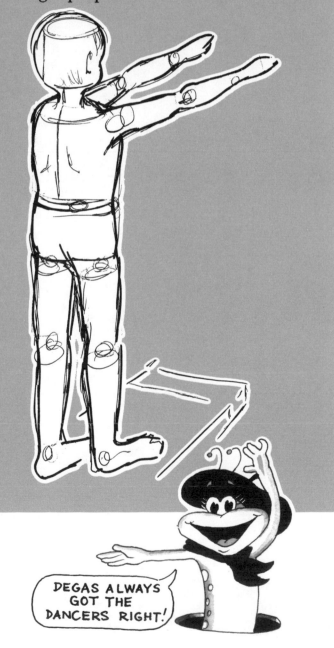

- Add an outline to show the finished shape. It is best to do this kind of drawing quickly.
- Do lots and lots of quick sketches.
- Try many different poses.

DEGAS ALWAYS GOT THE DANCERS RIGHT!

IS THERE A SKELETON IN YOUR CLOSET?

Probably not, but knowing something about the skeleton of the human body can be a help if you're serious about drawing people.

The skeleton is made up of all the bones in your body. (In fact, there are 206 of them.)

Knowing the shapes and the proportions of the bones and how they connect helps you to get the shape of the body right.

•Study a picture of the human skeleton. Try sketching the main bones. (Don't worry about detail. Just sketch quickly to get the shape.)

•Do lots and lots of sketches.

•Flesh out some of them to give you the human form.

ANNIGONI WAS A GREAT ONE FOR USING THE SKELETON!

IT'S NOT ONLY SKIN DEEP

With all of the practice you've had, you now know that it's really what goes on under the skin that counts. This is what gives things shape. It's time to try out your new skills.

- Start by drawing people around your house. Draw them doing ordinary things.
- Use different mediums (pencil, pastel, crayon, charcoal).
- Use different kinds of paper.
- Make some simple sketches and some more detailed ones.

WHY NOT SET UP A "PORTRAIT GALLERY" AND INVITE YOUR FRIENDS OVER TO VIEW IT?

DRAWING IT HOW IT *ISN'T*

So far, we've looked at how to draw lifelike figures. We've tried to make them look just like real life. Yet in art we can also draw people in ways that do not look so "real."

Some very famous artists used different styles to draw people.

Here are some figures sketched to resemble the way these artists drew.

SHE'S ACTUALLY TALKING ABOUT THREE ARTISTS: EL GRECO, MODIGLIANI, AND PICASSO!

LET'S FACE IT!

Faces tell us more about a person than almost anything. They can show their age, ethnic background (such as Chinese or Indian), gender (male or female), and mood (happy or sad).

• Start with your own face.
• Stand in front of a mirror and study the shape and proportion of your own face.

• Where do your ears start and finish?
• How wide apart are your eyes?
• What shape are your lips?
• How long is your neck?

•To sketch your face, start with an egg shape (an oval).

•Sketch in vertical and horizontal lines to show the general position of the eyes, the nose, and the mouth.

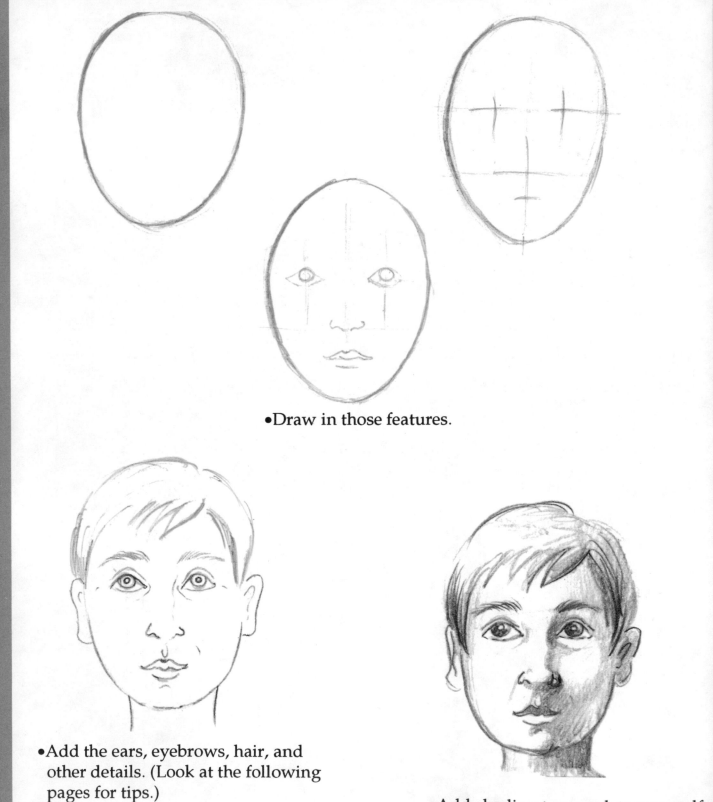

•Draw in those features.

•Add the ears, eyebrows, hair, and other details. (Look at the following pages for tips.)

•Add shading to complete your self-portrait.

GETTING AHEAD

Drawing faces will take lots of practice and you'll keep getting better at it.

- Ask someone to model for you.
- Is their head a true oval or is it rather squarish? Is it more rounded? When the head is tilted at an angle, notice how the features look different. Which feature is the strongest? Is it the eyes, the nose, the mouth?
- Sketch faces from many different angles.

LET'S FACE IT, WHISTLER WAS VERY FAMOUS AND HE DREW HIS MOTHER!

THE EYES HAVE IT

There are as many different eyes, noses, mouths, and ears as there are people in the whole world.

Eyes
- Start looking for the differences (the small ones, not just the big ones).
- Study faces while you're waiting for the bus, or sitting in the dentist's waiting room.
- Sketch lots and lots of facial features, showing different shapes, proportions, and sizes.

Mouths

• How wide is the mouth? Are the lips thick or thin?
Is the upper lip long or short? Check the distance from the upper lip to
the nose and find out.

Ears

When you start studying ears, the variety will amaze you.

Just keep practicing. Draw them all.

Noses

Noses are an important feature. • Use shading to show the shape.

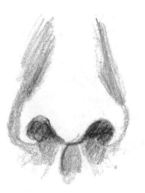

WHO KNOWS
WHY A NOSE
IS THE WAY IT IS?

HAIR! HAIR!

Hair makes a big difference to the way people look. (Just try putting on a wig!)

- Study hair – its length, its shape, its color, its texture, its thickness.
- Start sketching lots of different heads of hair. (Don't worry too much about features right now, just concentrate on the hair.)

LEONARDO DA VINCI MADE QUITE A FEATURE OF MONA LISA'S HAIR!

DO IT WITH FEELING

Our faces show how we feel. They show our emotions.

- Ask members of your family to pretend a whole range of emotions.
- Sketch their expressions.

- Use lines to show age as well as emotions.
- Use shading to help show the feelings.
- Try showing different emotions by sketching with simple lines.

- Practise over and over again.
  (Sketch while you're sitting in the car waiting for someone or while you're waiting to have your meal. Anytime!)

Once you've developed the basic skills, you can start to show "character" in faces. Character is more than a facial expression. When you see the portrait, you feel you know quite a lot about this person, such as their personality, mood, and age.

To help show character, focus on the most important facial feature. It could be a large nose (or a small one). It could be a high forehead or lots of wrinkles.

- Try using different mediums (pencil, crayon, charcoal, or pen and ink).

I'VE GOT TO HAND IT TO YOU!

Everyone's hands are different. They are as varied as faces!
Before you start drawing hands, spend time studying them.
•Start with your own. Let's get under your skin. Feel the bones. Feel
  where they start and where they end. Feel where they bend (the joints).
  You're feeling the skeleton of your hand.
The skeleton looks something like this sketch below. (Don't worry too
much about the details at this stage.)

 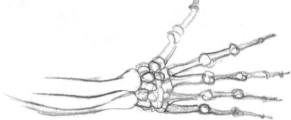

•Hold one of your hands in a "pose." With the other, lightly sketch the
  bones of your hand in position.

•Add an outline to make the shape.
•Use shading to "flesh it out."
•Add details, such as fingernails and
  wrinkles.

Study hands wherever you see them. What shape do they have?
Look at the length, shape, and thickness of fingers. Keep
practicing by drawing your own from different angles.

•First sketch the back of your hand.

•Now, sketch the palm of your hand.

•Draw your hand from a
  side-view, check out
  which finger is longest.

•Now, here's a challenge
  – a front-on view!

36

LISTENING TO HANDS

No, hands can't talk, but they do tell us a lot.
- Ask people who live with you to make their hands tell you what they are feeling.
- Sketch their hands. Use shading.

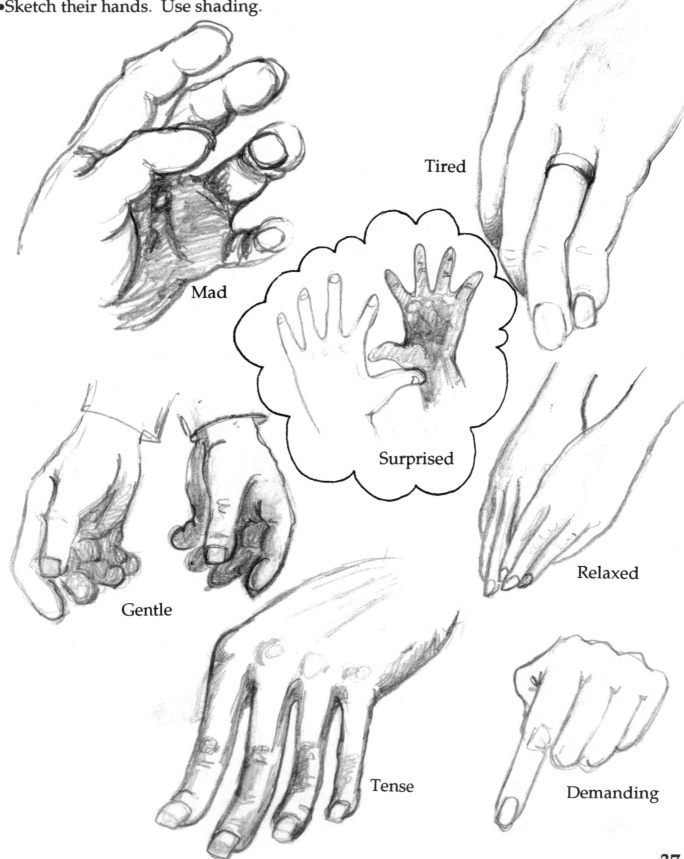

Mad

Tired

Surprised

Gentle

Relaxed

Tense

Demanding

PUT YOUR FOOT DOWN!

Use the same approach for feet as you did for hands.

•Feel your foot •Feel the bones

•Sketch the skeleton

•Add an outline

•Flesh it out

•Add details

Try drawing your own foot from different angles. Ask family members or friends to pose for you. You need to draw feet well if you want to show someone moving.

IT'S HARD TO FIND A FOOT IN PICASSO!

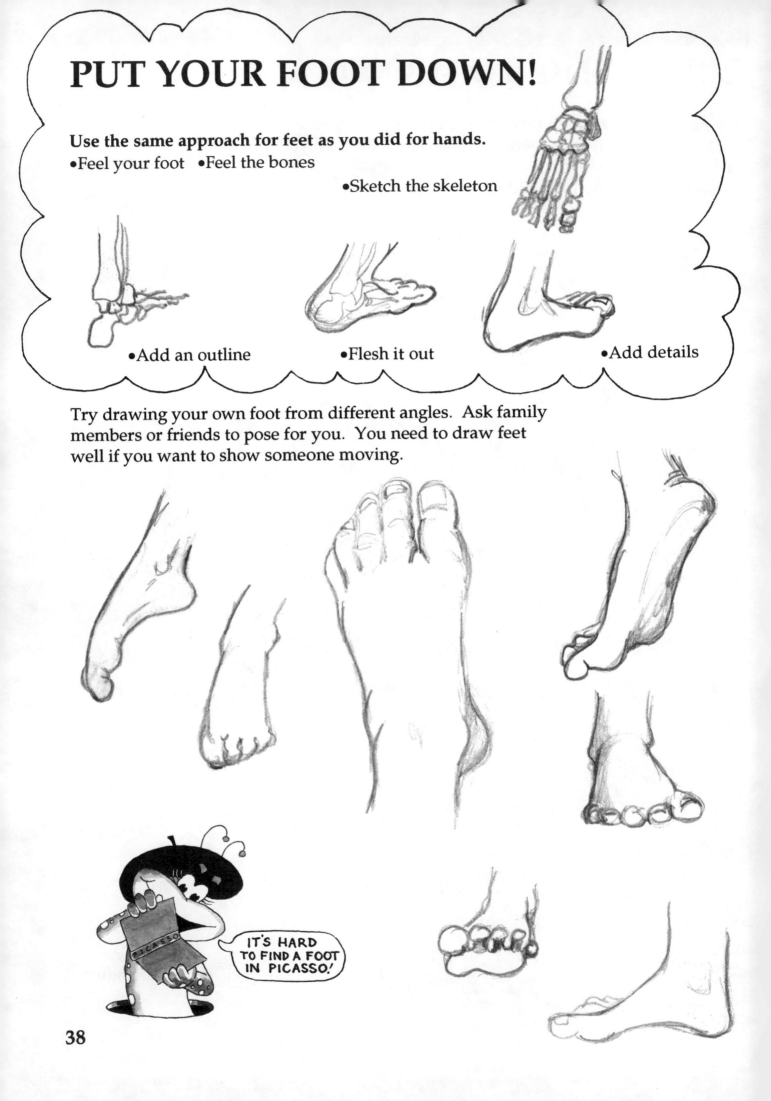

PUT YOUR FOOT IN IT!

Once you've got the basic shape of the foot mastered, you can add footwear to give character to people you draw.

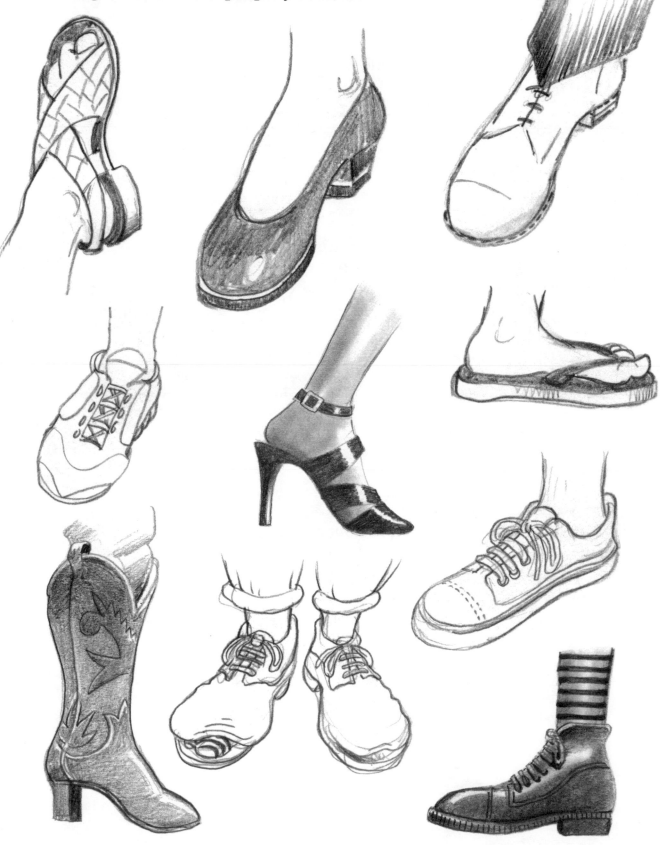

FRUITY SHAPES

If you want to draw fruit, you'll almost always start with either a circle or an oval – or a combination of both.

Let's start with an orange (or any round fruit you can find in the kitchen).
•First sketch the basic round shape.

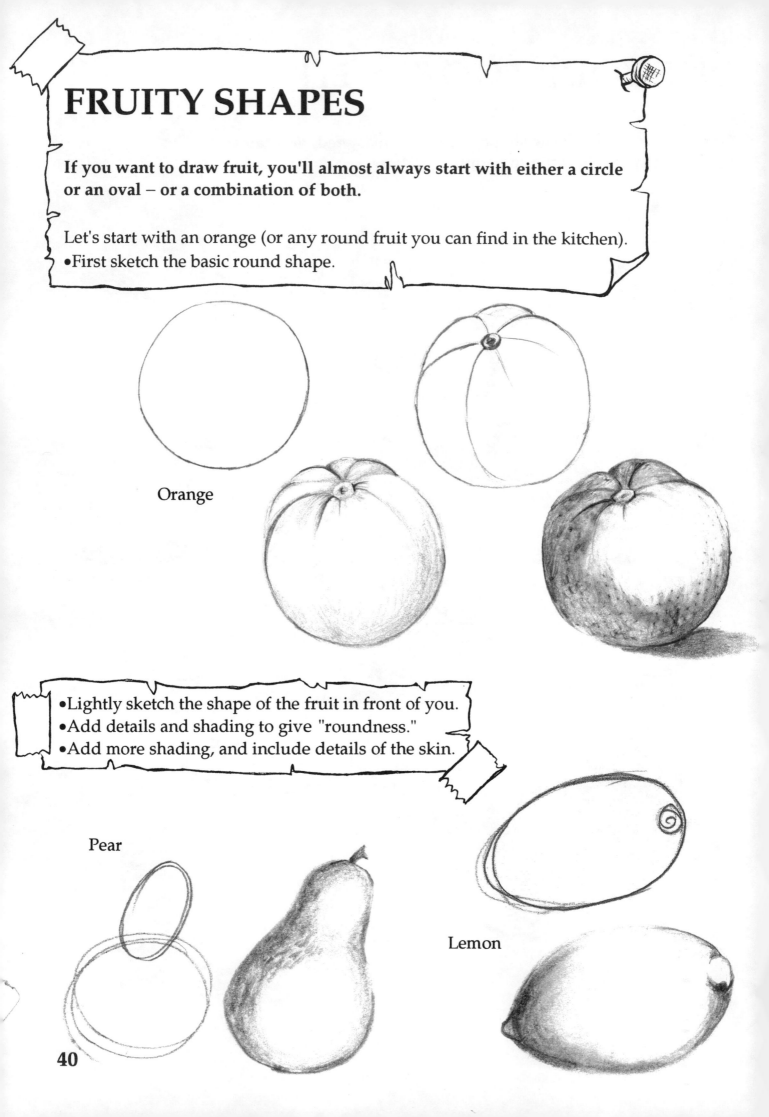

Orange

•Lightly sketch the shape of the fruit in front of you.
•Add details and shading to give "roundness."
•Add more shading, and include details of the skin.

Pear

Lemon

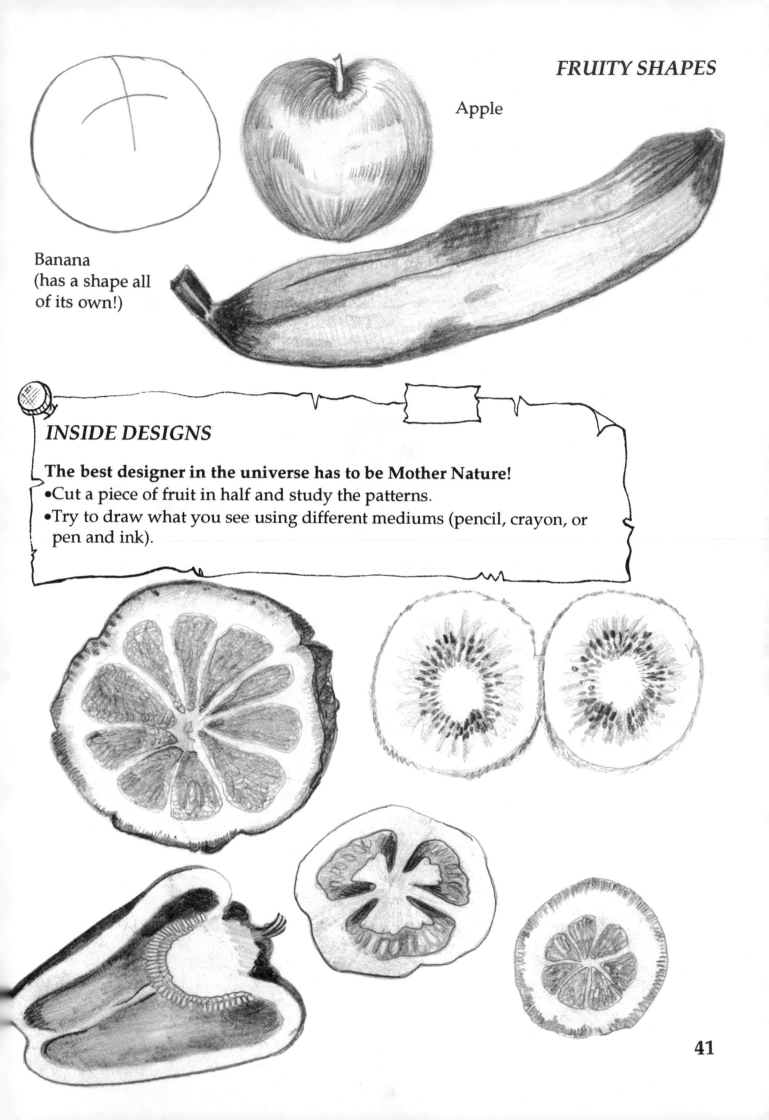

Apple

Banana
(has a shape all
of its own!)

INSIDE DESIGNS

The best designer in the universe has to be Mother Nature!
- Cut a piece of fruit in half and study the patterns.
- Try to draw what you see using different mediums (pencil, crayon, or pen and ink).

EAT YOUR VEGGIES

Borrow some of the vegetables in your kitchen. Notice how each vegetable has a basic shape: oval, round, oblong, and so on.
•Choose a medium that suits the vegetable you are going to draw.

•Look at the styles and mediums used below.

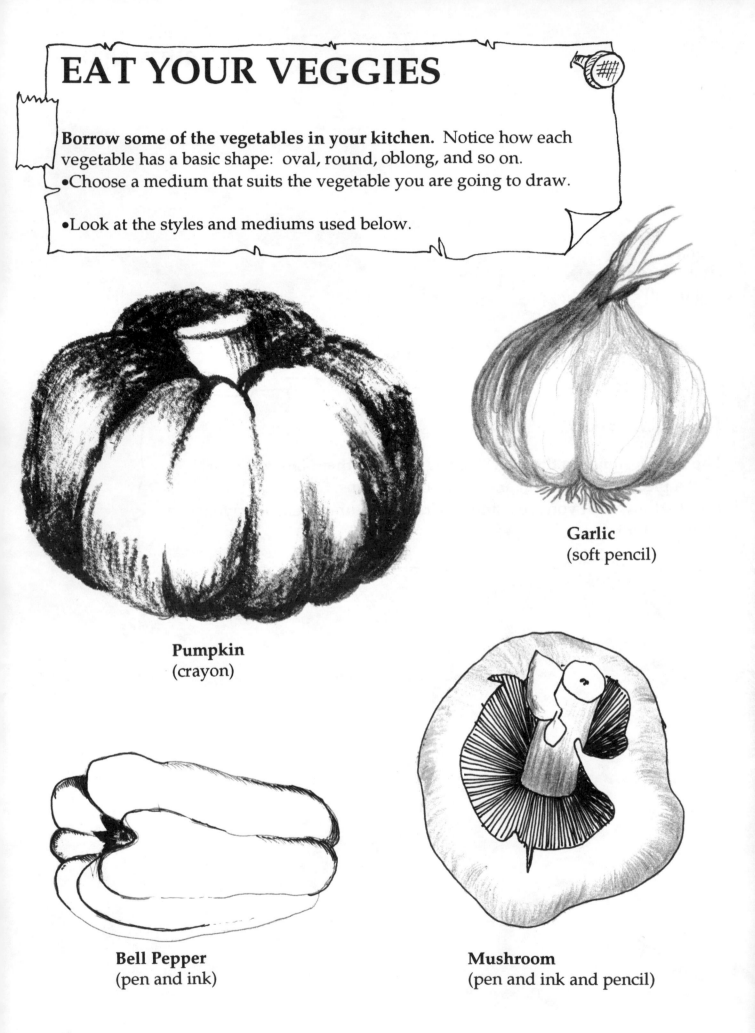

Pumpkin
(crayon)

Garlic
(soft pencil)

Bell Pepper
(pen and ink)

Mushroom
(pen and ink and pencil)

Have you ever sketched vegetables in your sketchbook?

Once you've practiced drawing single vegetables, try a bunch.

- Now "borrow" as many vegetables as you can from the refrigerator. Arrange them together as a group. Sketch the outline shape of the whole bunch and then work on each vegetable.
- Draw your picture three times using different mediums: pencil, pen and ink, and crayons.
- Use shading to show depth and texture.

Tomato
(charcoal)

HOW TO TREAT TREES

Trees – like everything else in nature – come in all shapes, sizes, colors, and textures.

•First, choose a tree to draw and sketch its outline.

•Next, think about the leaf shape. (You can't draw *every* leaf, but you can show lots of leaves by drawing them in clumps.)
•Now, add leaves and textures on the branches and trunk.

Try different mediums.
(You'll find that the *less detail* you show, the *farther away* the tree will seem.)

SOME PEOPLE CALL TREES "THE LUNGS OF A CITY." I WONDER WHY?

MILLION-DOLLAR FLOWERS

A painting of sunflowers done by a famous artist called van Gogh sold for millions of dollars. He started – just like you – by drawing one flower!

There are two basic ways to draw flowers:
•start at the center and "build" detail outward.

•or start by sketching an outline shape and then "fill in" the details.

ESCAPE INTO LANDSCAPE

A "landscape" is any part of the world around us. If it's the sea, you call it a "seascape."
Let's first look at rural (country) landscapes.

- Check your sketchbook for any scenes you've sketched of parks or gardens.
- Turn back to pages 8 to 11 ("Getting a Different Angle on It"). There we looked at composition or "framing up" our pictures.

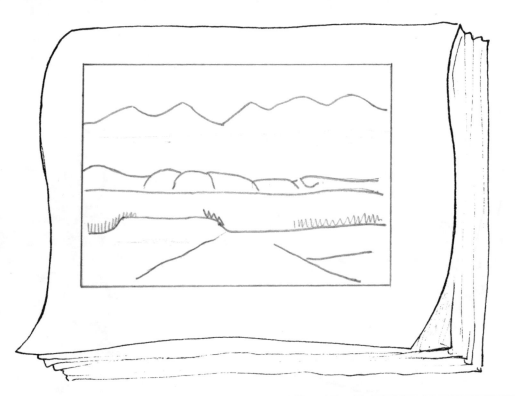

- Once you've framed the picture, sketch in the main shapes.
  If you add things in the front (foreground) of your picture, it will give depth to all the rest.

48

- Add details to your picture, starting at the back and working to the foreground.

Different mediums can give the same scene a very different feeling.

Pen and ink:
A seascape on a summer's day.

Charcoal:
The same place on a stormy day.

Try **pastel . . .**

or **crayon.**

REMEMBER REMBRANDT?

CITYSCAPES

Cityscapes are landscapes of towns and cities. If that's where you live, you'll have lots of ideas in your sketchbook.

Just look out your window.

•First sketch the basic skyline or the outline of roofs you see.

•Add more and more lines, one under the other.

•Now fill in some details (TV antennas, chimneys, windows).

•Make each house you draw a bit different.

Try using charcoal sideways to create building shapes. Add darker lines for details. (This makes the buildings look far away.)

Charcoal is good for concrete . . .   and for drawing bricks or paving stones.

To draw tall buildings such as skyscrapers, draw lots of rectangles.

Use different textures and details to add interest.

You usually have people in city (or urban) landscapes. Make crowds by drawing the shapes of people loosely with charcoal. Another way is to "scribble" your figures using loose lines.

Try drawing a scene putting all of these techniques together.

BREUGHEL PUT HUNDREDS OF PEOPLE INTO HIS PICTURES!

ANIMALS ARE PEOPLE TOO!

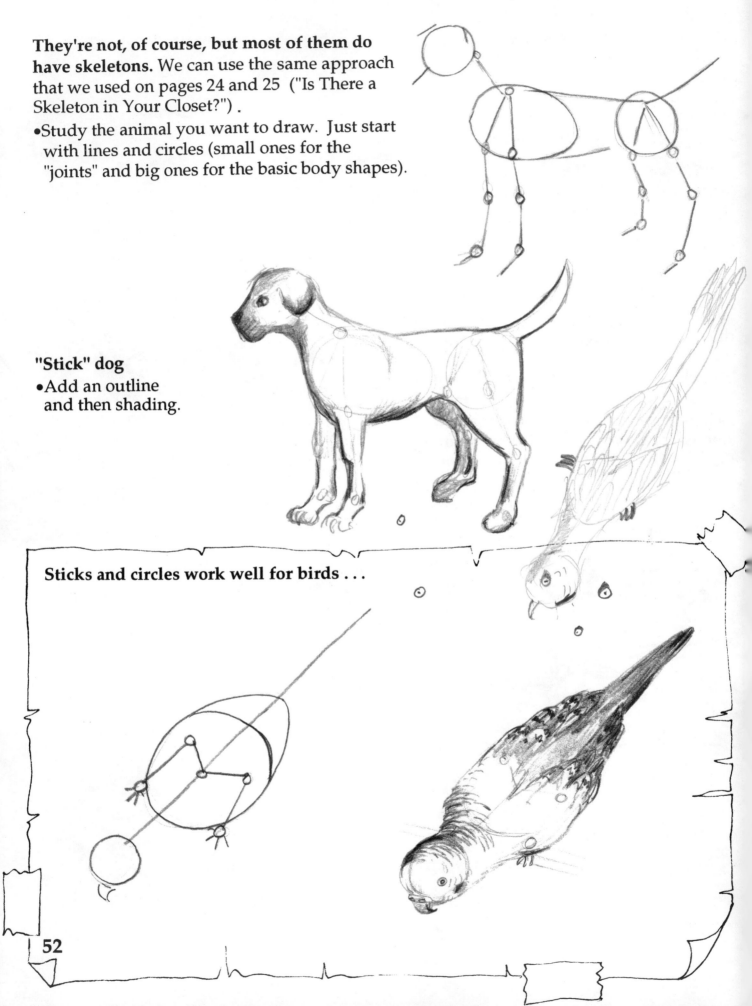

They're not, of course, but most of them do have skeletons. We can use the same approach that we used on pages 24 and 25 ("Is There a Skeleton in Your Closet?") .

- Study the animal you want to draw. Just start with lines and circles (small ones for the "joints" and big ones for the basic body shapes).

"Stick" dog
- Add an outline and then shading.

Sticks and circles work well for birds . . .

and koalas . . .
(Smudge the charcoal for a furry effect.)

and rabbits.
(Eyes are really important in animal drawings.)

Draw whatever pets you have at home or at school.

If you've got a cat, it's no use asking it to pose for you! It just won't stay still – unless it's asleep!

• Use really loose circular scribbles. Work fast and don't worry about details.
• Draw your cat stretching, running, climbing – in fact, doing all the things cats do.

DON'T HORSE AROUND!

Horses are very special animals to lots of people. They are fascinating to draw.

•The skeleton is a good place to start. Here's the basic bone structure of a horse. (It's *not perfect*, but who said it had to be? It's just to give us an idea!)

•Study a horse (or a picture of one).
•Get the proportions (sizes of different parts) right in your mind.
•Sketch a skeleton (or lines and circles).
•Draw the outline shape.
•Add shading to give depth and texture.

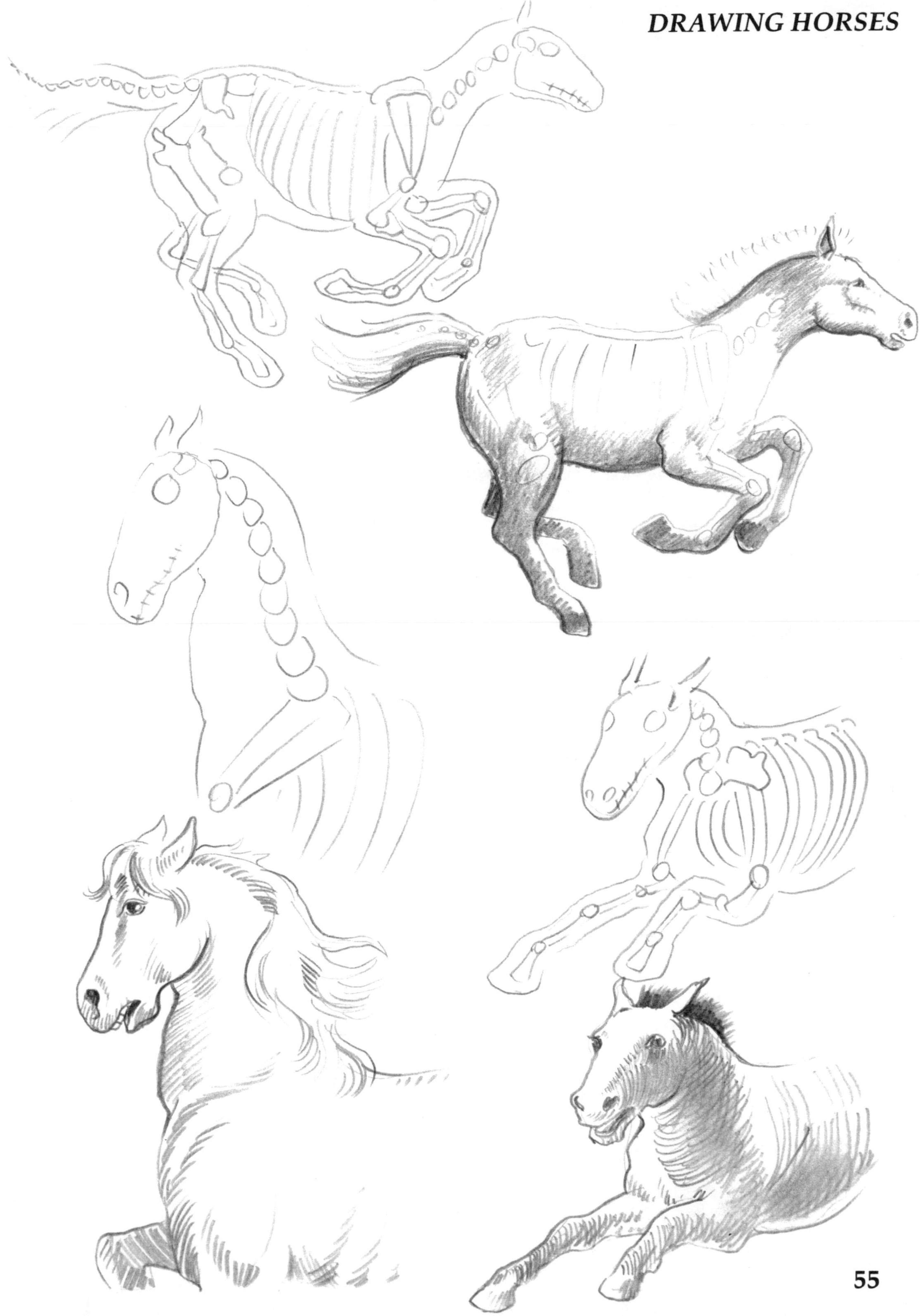

IT'S ALL IN THE FOLDS

Around your house you'll see lots of different kinds of fabrics: clothing, curtains, towels, chair coverings.

•Start looking carefully at fabrics. See how you can show different textures by using shading.

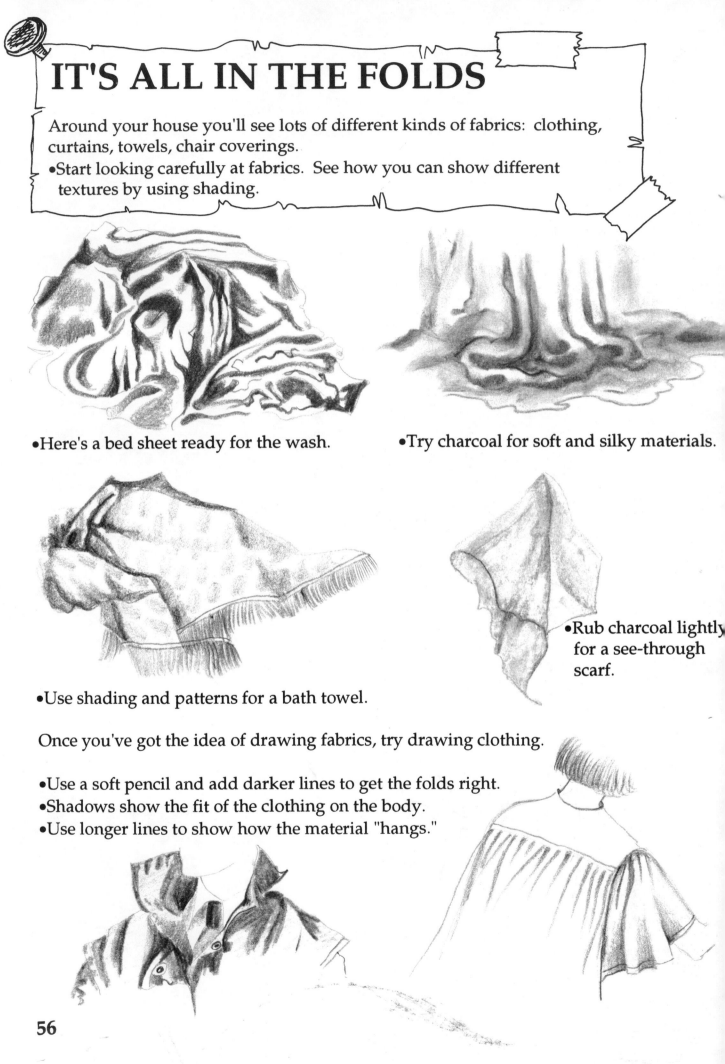

•Here's a bed sheet ready for the wash.

•Try charcoal for soft and silky materials.

•Rub charcoal lightly for a see-through scarf.

•Use shading and patterns for a bath towel.

Once you've got the idea of drawing fabrics, try drawing clothing.

•Use a soft pencil and add darker lines to get the folds right.
•Shadows show the fit of the clothing on the body.
•Use longer lines to show how the material "hangs."

MODELS THAT DON'T MOVE

A "still life" is a drawing of small objects – such as fruit or flowers in a vase. It's a great way to practice your drawing skills.

•Take a group of ordinary things you find around the house. Arrange them so that they look good. Before you start, study their basic shapes
•their perspective
•their different textures
•the shadows.

•Choose the medium you think will work best.

•Sketch and then add all the details that make a picture interesting.

Still-life pictures are even more interesting if you choose things with *very different* textures such as fabric, fruit, and glass.

Try doing the same still-life using different mediums.

TRAINS & PLANES & BOATS & CARS

When you think about it, the rules of drawing are very much the same whatever you plan to draw.

- First, study the basic shape.
- Sketch it using either boxes and cylinders or just an outline. Remember to use the idea of perspective. For a long train or truck, draw the lines back towards your vanishing point.

When you are happy with the basic shape, add as much detail as you like.

58

Once you've got the idea, you can start designing really fancy
trains, planes, boats, and cars.

• Draw things from different angles.
• Add extra details to make things look real.

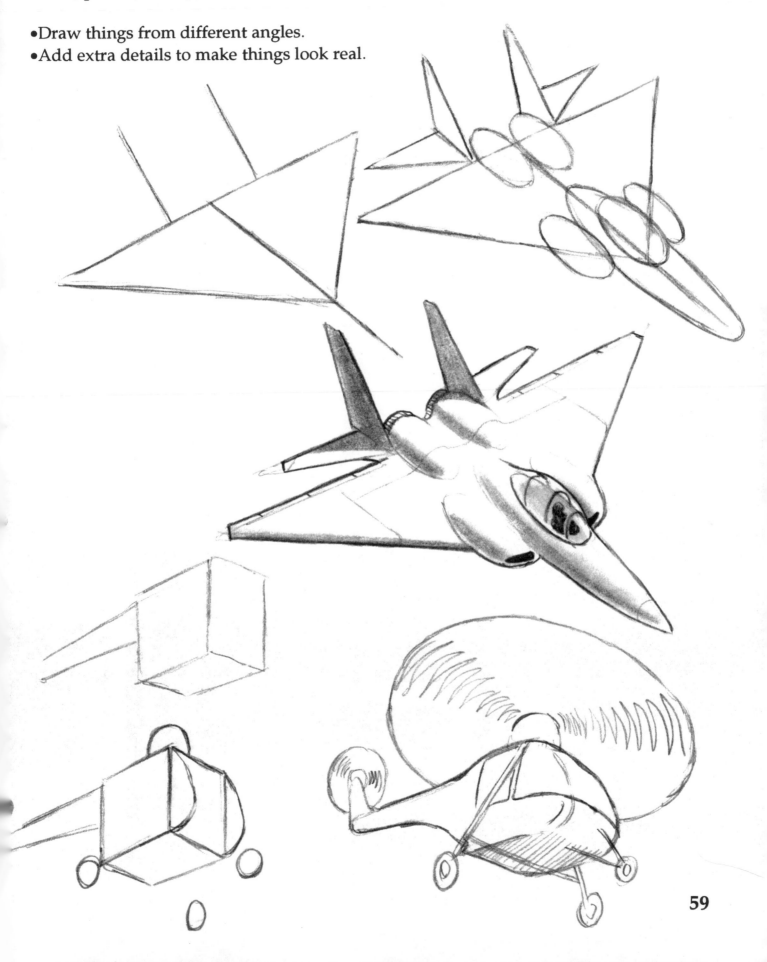

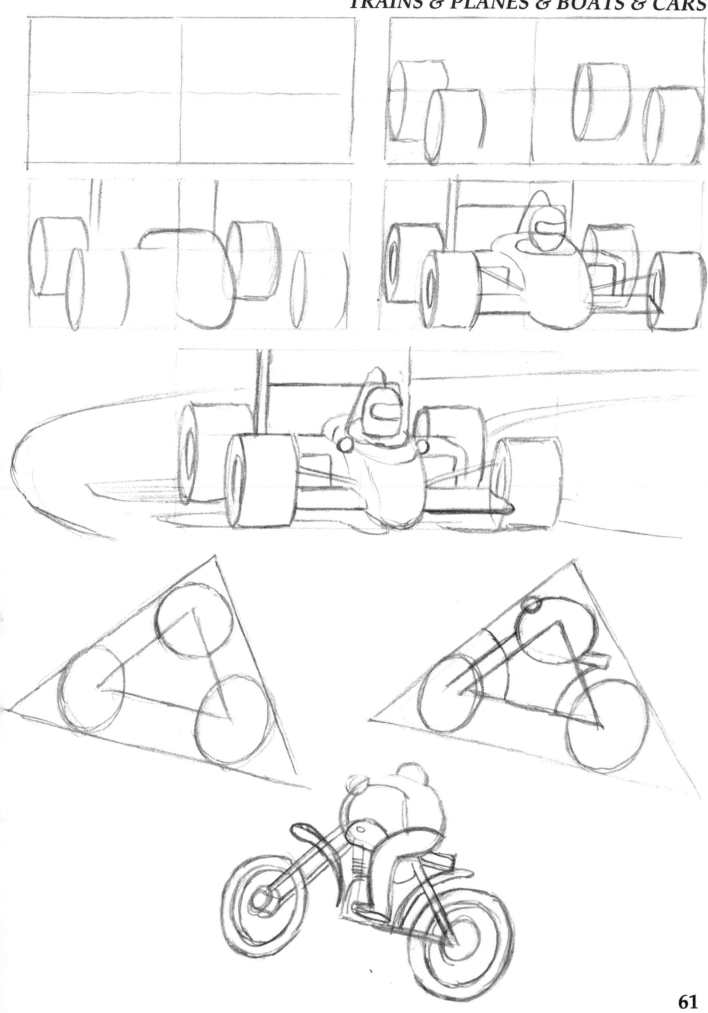

MOVE IT RIGHT ALONG!

**If you want your picture to really make an impression,
you can suggest movement.**
Say you want to give the impression of a great storm.
•Use dark, blurry lines.

This horse looks as if it's really bucking.
•Notice how few lines are used.

She's moving!
To give that impression,
the perspective has been
exaggerated. Her trunk
and arms have been drawn
to look way out in front
of her legs.

When you draw a skier from
below, you get the feeling
he's really jumping through
the air.

64